IMAGES
of America

ABALONE DIVING
ON THE
CALIFORNIA COAST

Susan Rebuck, age six, and Steve Rebuck, age nine, are in this c. 1956 photograph taken in Morro Bay, California, with "Black Fleet" abalone boats tied up. Susan, Steve, and a lot of other Morro Bay kids regularly ate abalone. At home, it could be abalone spaghetti, or at school, abalone sandwiches. Kids would trade their abalone sandwiches to the Japanese kids for peanut butter and jelly sandwiches—a good trade for everybody. (Photograph by Neva Rebuck.)

ON THE COVER: This image shows two Monterey Abalone Company boats at what is now Whalers Cove at Point Lobos State Parks. This was a staged picture for a local Monterey photographer. At the time, all the dive gear was new, as there are no dents in the helmets. (Courtesy of the Sandy Lydon collection.)

IMAGES
of America

ABALONE DIVING
ON THE
CALIFORNIA COAST

Steven L. Rebuck, Christopher Rebuck,
and Tim Thomas

ARCADIA
PUBLISHING

Published by Arcadia Publishing
Charleston, South Carolina

Printed in the United States of America

Library of Congress Control Number: 2023940843

For all general information, please contact Arcadia Publishing:
Telephone 843-853-2070
Fax 843-853-0044
E-mail sales@arcadiapublishing.com
For customer service and orders:
Toll-Free 1-888-313-2665

Visit us on the Internet at www.arcadiapublishing.com

CONTENTS

ACKNOWLEDGMENTS

First, we need to acknowledge all those who had the forethought to have a camera and photograph this wonderful history. We are fortunate to have these collections from various sources documenting the abalone fishery for the past 130-plus years.

Divers, academics, government scientists, and others were actively photographing and documenting the abalone fishery. One of these divers was Glen Bickford, an Iowa farm boy who came to California in 1936. Glen was soon photographing the commercial abalone fishery in California.

After World War II ended, there was a lot of former US military equipment available, sold at numerous war surplus stores. Glen and his associate, Alfred Hanson, another abalone diver, began rummaging through military surplus for cameras and lenses. They acquired movie cameras designed and used on World War II fighter planes. When fiberglass came along in the early 1950s, this team built underwater camera cases and began shooting film.

State abalone biologist J.B. Phillips and photographer Rey Ruppel documented research at Monterey during the 1930s. Another state biologist, Keith Cox, hired Glen Bickford and put together a team to investigate the abalone resource and fishery from Fort Bragg, Mendocino County, California, to Santa Catalina Island, Los Angeles County, California. This team produced *Fish Bulletin* 118, published by the Department of Fish and Game in 1962. Many of the images collected here were taken during this extensive research.

To assist the authors, Monterey Bay historians Kent Seavey and Dennis Copeland shared their knowledge. John Castagna of Monterey helped scan and organize. Janice House did a great job of scanning Glen Bickford's photographs and providing accurate metadata in the digital files. Author Tim Thomas appreciates his long friendship with diver Roy Hattori. We could not have completed this project without assistance from Peggy Mesler, owner of the Photo Shop in San Luis Obispo, California, and her technicians, Jeremy Baker and Trevor Gates. In addition, Erick Wand of Graphics by Erick, also of San Luis Obispo, assisted with organizing images and editing text.

INTRODUCTION

Abalone are large marine snails of the class Gastropoda, family Haliotidae. Worldwide, there are 140 identified species. In California, there are eight recognized species, with some sub-species and hybrids.

Besides humans, abalone are prey for octopus, starfish, crabs, and finfish. For many thousands of years, Native Californian peoples harvested abalone for sustenance and their beautiful shells. These shells were traded with other native tribes and can be found as artifacts all the way to the Mississippi River.

The name "abalone" comes from the Native people of Monterey, the Rumen, who called the red abalone "aulun." Spanish settlers called them "aulon." Over time, this became "abalone."

These early native harvesters of abalone also dove for them. We know this from human skulls with calcified ear canals. Vast shell piles—"middens," or kitchen areas—exist at many of the Southern California Channel Islands and on the mainland demonstrating the use of abalone and other shellfish for food.

Following the discovery of gold in California in 1849, many thousands of Chinese people were brought to California to work in the gold mines and build the railroad.

Some of these Chinese immigrants ended up in Monterey, where they observed the abundance of abalone on the nearshore. Although Spanish immigrants occupied the area, these Spanish people did not consume abalone, thinking it was affected by toxic algae common to filter-feeder shellfish. Abalone are grazers and so are not affected by toxic algae.

In China, only royalty and aristocrats were allowed to eat abalone. So, when these Chinese immigrants arrived and saw the abalone abundance, which was underutilized, they seized the opportunity and went fishing.

These Chinese immigrant fishermen began shore-picking abalone on wash rocks with wedges. They retrieved the abalone with a pole with a hook on it. They would dry the abalone through a series of cooking, blanching, washing, and sun drying. Next, the dried individual abalone were then either sliced with a knife and eaten, used as soup stock, or placed in burlap bags, loaded on Chinese junks (ships), and shipped to the Orient.

By 1895, Japanese immigrants had also discovered the abalone beds at Monterey. A Japanese national, Otosobura Noda, who was then working as a labor contractor for the Pacific Improvement Company, the landowner arm of Union Pacific Railroad, noticed the abundance of abalone in Monterey Bay. Noda referred to the "carpet of abalone."

In October 1897, the Japanese government sent Gennosuke Kodani, who was in the dried abalone business in the Chiba Prefecture of Japan to Monterey, California, to investigate. Kodani identified Whalers Cove at Point Lobos, south of Monterey, as the site for drying and canning abalone. In 1898, Kodani sent for divers—Kodani's younger brother Nakajira Kodani, Ichinosuke Yasuda, Daisuke Yasuda, and Rinja Yamamoto were all Ama divers.

Abalone were also fished in Japan; the common name was "awabi." However, when these Ama divers began diving at Monterey, the water, typically 45-55 degrees, was too cold for the traditional cotton dress. These "sake barrel divers," named as such for the sake barrels they used as floats, needed better and warmer equipment.

Heavy diving gear had been invented between 1820 and 1850 and was being used in Japan. Kodani had heavy diving gear shipped to Monterey, and these divers were soon fishing the offshore reefs from small boats. Kadani selected Whalers Cove at Point Lobos as the spot to deliver and process abalone. Kodani went into business at Point Lobos with Alexander McMillen Allan and created an abalone meat drying and canning facility.

Since there were few local markets for abalone, most abalone was shipped to Asia, Hawaii, and Australia, where there were large Japanese and Chinese populations.

Heavy gear weighs approximately 150 pounds, but in the water, the suit retains air, so it can float. The diver has a valve in his helmet that he can use to release air or to inflate the suit and return to the surface. Inside the rubberized canvas suit, the diver wears layers of wool; even when wet, wool keeps one warm. Air was sent to the diver using hand-operated pumps and, later, gasoline engines were used to power air compressors.

In 1913, the State of California banned the export of dried abalone, followed by a ban on drying abalone in 1915. Also, in 1915, canning was limited to one-pint cans, followed by a ban on canning in 1917. By the 1920s, concerns about overfishing brought about more conservation laws that affected the existing diving and marketing of abalone. First, laws prohibiting abalone fishing inside 20 feet sea water from the low-tide mark inshore restricted access to the Chinese divers. Next, bans on canning created hardship for everyone in the abalone business. The Chinese reacted by shifting abalone fishing to the backside of the Channel Islands where little observation occurred. But soon, a new way of processing would evolve.

In 1907, Ernest "Pop" Doelter moved his family to Monterey. At first, Pop specialized in serving oysters. Pop was of German descent; a restaurateur familiar with processing meat like schnitzel. Pop began experimenting with how to process and prepare abalone. He cut the raw meat into steaks. Afterward, he pounded the steaks to tenderize them.

Pop's abalone recipe included dredging them in egg, followed by breadcrumbs, and then cooking them quickly. Pop introduced his "abalone steaks" in San Francisco in 1913. His big breakthrough came in 1915 when he introduced abalone steaks at the Panama–Pacific International Exhibition.

Pop Doelter had taken a product described as "like eating rubber" and transformed it into an international epicurean delight. Demand for fresh abalone steaks expanded.

Soon, people were coming to Café Ernest in Monterey to eat fresh abalone. He was soon serving abalone steaks, abalone stew, abalone chowder, and abalone nectar, which is the juice that came out of the meat. The local newspaper began calling Pop Doelter "the Abalone King." People from all over the world were coming to the Café Ernest for abalone dinners. Many would leave songs and poetry in the guest book:

> Oh! Some folks boast of quail on toast,
> Because they think it's tony;
> But I'm content to owe my rent
> And live on abalone

By the late 1920s, another group of divers entered the fishery at Morro Bay, California. The Pierce family were of Salinan Indian and Welch heritage. The eldest brother, William "Bill" Pierce, had been harvesting Pismo clams at Morro Bay, where he was known as "Clam Digger Billy." Not long after that, he would be known as "Abalone Bill."

At first, in 1928, the brothers worked off the beach with Bill Pierce, wearing 150 pounds of gear and walking into the surf. By the next season, they reportedly had a boat.

Soon, other families at Morro Bay entered the abalone fishery: the Brebes family and the Sylvester family were Portuguese people via the Azore Islands. The Montgomery family moved to Morro Bay in 1933 from Texas. The Reviea family also came from Texas in 1927. The Reviea and Pierce families were connected by marriage.

Other fisheries to the south opened up, fishing other varieties of abalone, including pink, green, white, and black abalone. By 1948, the Pierce Brothers Fisheries had moved its processing to Stearns Wharf in Santa Barbara, California, and its fishing operation to the Northern Channel Islands.

During World War II, Al Hanson and Barney Clancy worked at the Keiser Shipyard in Hayward, California, building Liberty ships. They learned about heavy-gear diving at Keiser. Hanson purchased some dive gear and would retrieve lost tools and parts for extra money.

Hanson drove down to Ragged Point one day, the San Luis Obispo/Monterey County line, to watch Bill Pierce dive. The plan was for Hanson to buy Pierce's boat. Unfortunately, the air hose of Pierce was "wrapped" in the propeller that day. Nobody on the boat knew how to swim, and Pierce drown.

Following this life lesson, Al Hanson installed "bail-out bottles" on his weight belt. This bottle of compressed air would inflate the dive suit should the air hose be cut. He also installed "check valves" in the helmets to stop air from escaping as well as stainless steel cable in the air hose. These modifications would save many lives. The human body is 75 percent liquid, and when the air hose is cut, one's body essentially liquefies, and the liquid races up the hose.

In an interesting footnote for Al Hanson's underwater camera development with Glen Bickford, Al Hanson would go on to sell motion picture film to Walt Disney and an appearance in *20,000 Leagues Under the Sea* as a stuntman for Kirk Douglas and diver technical consultant.

Barney Clancy, another Midwestern transplant, founded Veterans Fisheries and created his own fleet of dive boats, "the Black Fleet." When Clancy and Hanson left Cambria, California, Clancy relocated to Wilmington near Long Beach, California, and Hanson went to Santa Catalina Island, Los Angeles County, California.

By the 1950s, seafood markets expanded, and seafood restaurants prospered. At Morro Bay, Brebes Ocean House became one of several processing houses for abalone. Situated on the Morro Bay Embarcadero, Frank Brebes, who was also a diver, offered a place to unload, process, and market the abalone. Brebes even had a large area where abalone boats were hauled out and would undergo maintenance during the closed summertime season.

Other Morro Bay abalone processors were Betty Jameson, Harold and Rosie Elmore, Morro Bay Abalone Company, Rosie Montgomery Whitlock, Queen of the Sea Brand, and Chuck and Don Sites.

Between the 1940s and 1960s, the sea otter in California, *Enhydra lutris*, had been slowly expanding its population and range, southward from Monterey County into San Luis Obispo County. By the early 1960s, sea otter foraging was depleting much of the abalone grounds north of Morro Bay. As landing declined, many of the older divers retired. Some, including the younger men, moved south to Santa Barbara, where they could fish the mainland, north and south, plus the northern and southern Channel Islands.

In the early 1960s, the Radon family moved to Morro Bay from Oklahoma. Ron Radon Sr. had new ideas about boat building. New technologies called "out-drives" were invented. This was a transmission and propeller once mounted to an engine now mounted in the stern (rear) of the boat. A live well was built into the hull where abalone could be stored during the fishing trip. These boats were smaller and could now be operated by two-man crews (five men in the Japanese era, and three after that). This boat revolutionized the dive fishery, which, by the early 1970s, included sea urchin diving. Ron's sons Mike, Don, and Ron Jr. would build their careers diving abalone and building boats. Radon Boats continues at Goleta, California.

During World War II, Underwater Demolition Teams (UDT; later, US Navy SEALs) began "swim diving" along with walking. This was followed by equipment invention; for example, self-contained underwater breathing apparatus (SCUBA), wet suits, and fins revolutionized commercial diving. Recreational fishermen also enjoyed fishing abalone for subsistence and fun.

This unique fishing history continued until the State of California closed the abalone fisheries, commercial and recreational, south of San Francisco, due to declining resources in 1997. Black abalone became an endangered species in 2009. White abalone became an endangered species in 2001. In 2017, the State of California closed the sport-only fishery north of San Francisco. The northern abalone stocks began declining about 2010. An increase in purple urchin populations was also occurring. Kelp disappeared, and abalone starved. As of this writing, no studies have been published to identify what occurred to Northern California abalone and ecology.

In the 1960s, some of the divers were still young enough to continue their diving careers, as other opportunities arose. For some of the divers in Santa Barbara, energy production companies were building offshore oil platforms at Summerland, California, just south of Santa Barbara, California.

These early projects were in approximately 100 feet sea water. This was in the range of depth where compressed air diving could be conducted safely. But soon, there were plans to go out deeper.

The US Navy had experimented with what would become "mix gas diving" but had never perfected this technology. Along came a large group of seasoned divers, former abalone divers, with new ideas. On November 3, 1962, former abalone divers Hugh "Danny" Wilson and Laddie Handelman produced the first successful dive to 400 feet sea water offshore of Santa Barbara, California. These divers used a 20 percent oxygen/80 percent helium mixture. Another abalone diver, Robert Ratcliffe, designed a manifold where a technician could adjust the air/gas mix as a diver descended or ascended. This event spawned a whole new way to get things done in deep ocean water.

The next step in this evolution was to utilize a former scientific machine: the Bathysphere. It was developed in 1928–1929 by Otis Barton and made famous by William Beebe, who, on August 15, 1934, made a dive to 3,028 feet sea water.

Soon after their 400-foot dive, Handelman and his group of abalone divers founded Cal Dive in Santa Barbara, California. These men recognized the Bathysphere (diving bell) could also be used for commercial work. Cal Dive developed a Bathysphere that would transport divers to their working depth. Next, the divers swam out through a hatch at the bottom of the bell. Once the first diver had completed his task or run out the clock, he would re-enter the bell, and the second diver would swim out and do his task. When the time was up, a technician would pressurize the bell to its working depth and bring the men back to the surface. Still under pressure, the men were connected to another chamber, in which they would live for up to three weeks at a time. There are now working dives to over 1,000 feet sea water.

The problem, which affects not only divers, but also miners and tunnel builders, is atmospheric pressure. For every 33 feet one goes below the surface, another atmosphere of pressure is placed on one's body.

Nitrogen gas in one's body is compressed during a dive. If one surfaces rapidly, the nitrogen gas expands. If there is a bubble of nitrogen in one's brain or spinal cord, the bubble increases in size and ruptures tissue. Paralysis and/or death may occur. What mixed gas does is eliminate the troublesome nitrogen and replace it with inert helium.

This malady, "caissons disease," is also commonly called "the bends," derived from the afflicted diver's body being bent over. At very deep depths, contemporary divers may experience being "helium bent."

Because of these inventions, in the 1960s, Cal Dive was involved with training US astronauts for their missions in space. Divers worked with Astronauts in a weightless environment. After Cal Dive, came Oceaneering International, Inc., founded by many of the same individuals, who were mostly former abalone divers. Oceaneering Space Solutions is now engaged with NASA in building space suits and helmets for the US trip to Mars, modeled after the Robert Ratcliffe "Rat Hat."

One

HISTORIC HUMAN USE OF ABALONE

Along many areas of the California coast are Native American middens (or kitchens), where animals, including abalone, were processed for food. This photograph is of one of those middens at Santa Rosa Island, Santa Barbara County, California, one of the Channel Islands. One of the abalone shells from this midden was recovered at a depth of 12 feet and was estimated to be 6,800 years old. (Santa Barbara Museum of Natural History, California Department of Fish and Game.)

This Indian cemetery at Santa Rosa Island contained abalone shells radiocarbon dated to be 7,070 years old. Several skeletons measuring over seven feet were found. The tops of these skulls were painted red. (California Department of Fish and Game.)

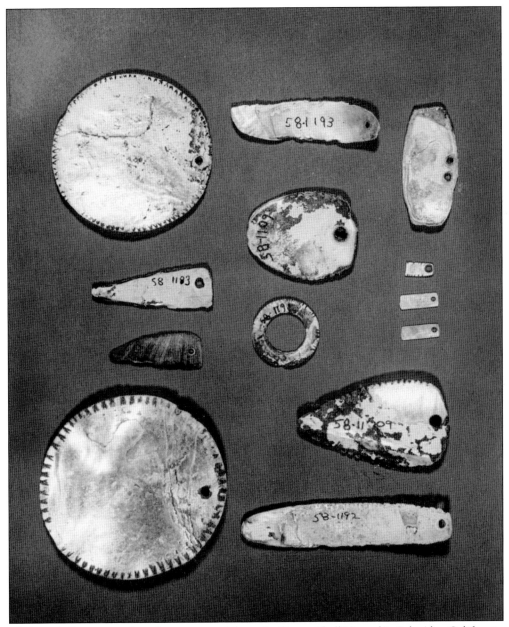

Abalone shell money and artifacts recovered from the Castro Shell Mound in Palo Alto, California, are estimated to be 1,500 years old. (Stanford University, California Department of Fish and Game.)

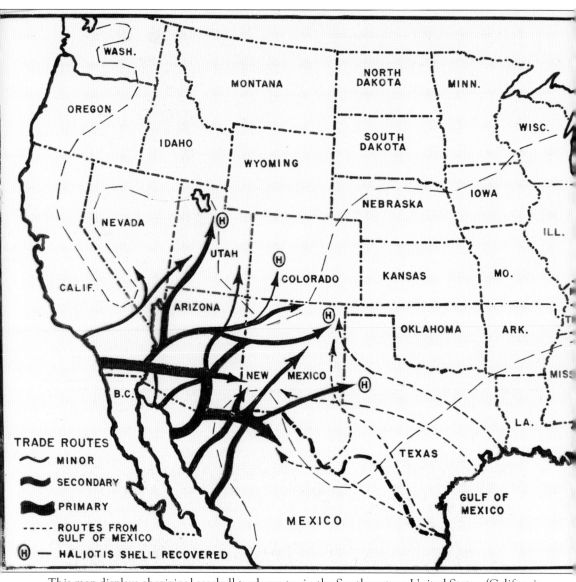

This map displays aboriginal seashell trade routes in the Southwestern United States. (California Department of Fish and Game.)

People have been fishing and diving for abalone in the Monterey Bay area for thousands of years. Monterey was the ancestral home of the Rumsen Native peoples of Monterey. A native culture can be traced to the Monterey Bay area about 10,000 years ago, and they made their living fishing the bay. This piece is known as *Monterey Women*; the artist is unknown.

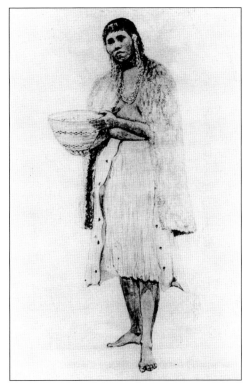

Even the word "abalone" comes from the Rumsen people. "Aulun" is a word for the red abalone, the largest and predominant abalone found in Monterey Bay, and linguists have traced it and "abalone" all the way back to Monterey. The artist of this sketch is Linda Yamane.

The Rumsen were the first abalone divers in Monterey Bay—a fact known from ancient burials recently found. The men have what is commonly called "surfer's ear," a small bony growth that covers the eardrum, indicating they spent a lot of time in the cold waters of Monterey Bay. This art is by Linda Yamane.

Chinese fishermen began arriving in Monterey in the early 1850s, and it was abalone that brought them. Word spread quickly to the California Chinese community resulting in what one San Francisco newspaper referred to, in 1857, as the "abalone rush." By 1879, more than four million pounds of red abalone had been harvested by Chinese fishermen. (California History Room, Monterey Library.)

A group of Japanese businessmen called themselves the Japanese Association, established in 1908 when this photograph was taken. These men were mostly all associated with the Monterey fishing industry, primarily abalone, and the Monterey Wharf. The man on the lower right is Otosaburo Noda, a leader in the community responsible for creating the Monterey abalone fishery. (California History Room, Monterey Library.)

Gennosuke Kodani was in the abalone business in the Chiba Prefecture of Japan. When he first arrived in Monterey in October 1897, he was so impressed with what he saw, he immediately sent for abalone divers known as ama to come to Monterey to quickly capitalize on this abundance. (Kodani family collection.)

On December 3, 1897, the Japanese government issued passports to Nakajiro Kodani, the younger brother to Gennosuke and a trained marine biologist, and Ichinosuke Yasuda, Daisuke Yasuda, and Rinji Yamamoto, all ama divers. Arriving in Monterey in late December, they immediately began to dive for abalone in Monterey Bay. (Kodani family collection.)

Kodani spent some time looking for the perfect place for his abalone fishing business and stumbled upon Point Lobos about 10 miles south of Monterey. He was so impressed by how much it looked like Japan, he immediately negotiated with the owner, Alexander McMillian "A.M." Allan, to lease a small portion of the property. This image was taken around 1895. (Kodani family collection.)

The Point Lobos
Canning Co.
INCORPORATED.

DEEP SEA ABALONE
Monterey, Cal.

After watching Kodani and his abalone operations for about a year, Allan invested in the company, and they became partners. Allan was a mining engineer and racetrack designer. He came to Monterey and Point Lobos because he was part owner of a coal mine there. The coal proved to be of a low grade, and the company decided to sell Point Lobos. Allan thought he could do something with the property and bought it from his partners. (Tom Fordham collection.)

Together, Kodani and Allan established a unique business and pioneered deep-diving techniques before unseen in California. Here, Kodani stands in a pile of red abalone shells at Point Lobos. (Kodani family collection.)

Two ama are dressed in their traditional ama gear which consists, of a white cotton outfit, abalone basket (knit bag), abalone pry wrapped around the waist, and a pair of goggles that originally had pigs' bladders attached to them that they would squeeze to help release the pressure. These amas would dive 30 to 40 feet, holding their breath for up to four minutes. (Kodani family collection.)

By the turn of the century, the Japanese began to use helmet gear. This was far more efficient and, more importantly, warmer. The water temperatures in Monterey Bay are about 15 degrees colder than in the Chiba Prefecture of Japan. The dive gear came from Japan and included long john–type underwear made of thick wool. (California History Room, Monterey Library.)

Here are two abalone boats at Point Lobos in about 1900. Rather than bring boats from Japan or take the time to build new ones, the Japanese abalone companies took some abandoned Portuguese whaling boats left at Point Lobos and converted them for their use diving abalone. They added a large copperplate to the side of the boat so, when pulling up abalone baskets, they would not scrape the boat. (California History Room, Monterey Library.)

This is diver Toyomatsu Yamaguchi, who came to Monterey in 1908. Many of the Monterey divers came from the Chiba Prefecture in an area called Minamiboso. People have been diving abalone there for centuries. In the early part of the 20th century around the Minamiboso area, there was a disease killing off the brown kelp that abalone feeds on. Because of that, there was no abalone to dive for. Divers had to go elsewhere to find work so they could care for and feed their families, and many came to Monterey. (Yamaguchi family collection.)

This is diver Chomatsu Kawakami, who first came to Monterey in 1907. In Japan, he was a rice farmer and not a diver. Within a day of arriving in Monterey, with no training whatsoever, he was diving abalone—he hated it, but he ended up living in Monterey for 20 years. Eventually, his son also became a diver in Monterey. (Kawakami family collection.)

By the turn of the 20th century, there was a lot of suspicion about the Monterey Japanese abalone industry. After all, no one in Monterey was eating it. The Japanese were drying it and shipping it to Asia. In 1905, the Japanese defeated the Russian military in the Japanese-Russo War. In 1908, a news story appeared in newspapers across the United States with the headline "Yellow Spies work Frisco." What the story suggests is that the Japanese were not collecting abalone but in fact were mapping the Monterey Bay to prepare for the Japanese Army to land at Santa Cruz, about 40 miles north of Monterey, and march over the Santa Cruz mountains and take the city of San Francisco! (Above; Monterey Library/California History Room, Collection Natural History Museum/ Smithsonian Collection; below Monterey JACL Heritage Center/Museum.)

One of the dive boats is seen at Point Lobos in about 1909. The two men on the left are Chomatsu Kawakamu and Toyomatsu Yamaguchi; Gennosuke Kodani is standing right behind Yamaguchi. The hand pump can be seen in the middle. All the diving gear, including the pump, was imported from Japan. (Kodani family collection.)

In April 1930, A.M. Allan died. The Japanese divers and their families were so appreciative of Allan's support and friendship, they held a memorial service for him at the Chosho-ji Temple in Shirahama Village in Japan. Nakajiro Kodani is sitting at the far right, and Chomatsu Kawakami is standing right behind him. (Kawakami family collection.)

This is a celebratory coat, called a Mawai, which was given to Japanese fishermen at the end of a very good season. This one is unique. There are only two of these known to exist today, with one in a museum in Japan and the other on exhibit at the Monterey JACL (Japanese American Citizens League) Heritage Center. (Monterey JACL Collection.)

This is a label for canned abalone from the Monterey Abalone Company, Kodani and Allan's company. This was an attempt to sell abalone to the Western markets. The abalone was diced and steamed in the cans like other canned fish products at that time. (Kodani family collection.)

Here, a Monterey Japanese abalone boat pulls the dive boat at Point Lobos. The cannery where abalone was canned can be seen on the far left. Note the American flag on the stern of the dive boat. (Kodani family collection.)

"Pop" Ernest Doelter, the Abalone King, stands in a pile of abalone shells near his restaurant on the Monterey Wharf. Pop would give these shells away, and people would line their gardens with abalone or inlay the shell into the walls that surrounded them. (Pat Sands collection.)

Pop Doelter, a German restaurateur, moved with his family to Monterey in 1907 and opened a small European-style restaurant called the Café Ernest. Pop stands in the doorway of his Café Ernest. (Pat Sands collection.)

This advertisement for the Café Ernest appeared in a local Monterey publication right after he first opened his restaurant in 1907. Toke Point oysters were his specialty. The oysters came by train every day from San Francisco. Oysters, like any shellfish, do not stay fresh for long, and often, his oysters would arrive spoiled. He was always looking for something new to offer at his restaurant. (Tim Thomas collection.)

CELEBRATED
"Toke Point" Oysters
Cafe Ernest
Stew or Fry 30c.
441 ALVARADO ST.

Here is an early image inside the Café Ernest around 1908. It is here that Pop invented the abalone steak. He brought some fresh abalone into his kitchen, pulled it from its shell, sliced the foot, pounded it with a wooden mallet to break up the connective tissue, dredged it through some egg wash and cracker crumbs, and cooked it up quickly in butter and olive oil. Soon, folks were coming from all over to eat fresh abalone steaks in Pop's Café Ernest. (California History Room, Monterey Library.)

Bohemians began moving to the Monterey Peninsula after the 1906 San Francisco earthquake and fire. Led by George Sterling, "the King of the Bohemians," they would often picnic on Carmel Beach, and the main feature would be an abalone stew. To help pass the time, these poets would recite abalone ditties as they pounded the abalone. (Pat Sands collection.)

These bohemians would visit the Café Ernest for abalone steak dinners and write those abalone ditties they created on Carmel Beach while pounding abalone in Pop's guestbook. This is a page from August 28, 1913, where several of these ditties can be seen. Jack London was the first to publish many of the verses of the "Abalone Song" in his 1913 book *The Valley of the Moon*. (Pat Sands collection.)

31

In 1913, Pop was offered a job and the opportunity to bring his abalone recipes to San Francisco at a restaurant called the Hof Bräu. He was offered so much money that he packed up his family and his abalone recipes and moved to San Francisco. This is the very first time that abalone appeared on a printed menu. (California Historical Society Collection.)

However, even in sophisticated San Francisco, abalone was a tough sell, as it was something new. This advertisement appeared in the *San Francisco Chronicle* at least once a week. (Tim Thomas collection.)

Pictured is the interior of the home of Chomatsu Kawakami in the village of Shirahama. Many of the Monterey divers came from this small village, and their families to this day still have these shrines honoring their loved ones who traveled so far to risk their lives diving abalone. The abalone shells came out of Monterey Bay well over 100 years ago. (Kodani family collection.)

In February 1915, the Panama–Pacific International Exhibition world's fair opened, the whole world came to San Francisco, and abalone was on the menu. In the Monterey County exhibit, the Monterey Abalone Company gave out free cans of Monterey abalone as a souvenir and told visitors of the Hof Bräu restaurant where one could get a full abalone steak dinner. (Kodani family collection.)

Pop Ernest's

372 Bush Street — Between Kearny and Montgomery

A place to eat — morning, noon and night. Specializes on sea food, game and poultry. Big deep sea mussels as not known before in San Francisco. Exclusive: Abalone a'la Ernest in various solid and liquid forms. Pop is recognized as the discoverer of Abalone as a white man's delicacy.

Business Lunch 11-2, 35 Cents

Soon, the whole world wanted this new seafood sensation. Pop quit his job at the Hof Bräu and opened a new restaurant just a few blocks away, naming it Pop Ernest's. By 1917, there was a great deal of anti-German sentiment in the United States. Frankfurters became hot dogs, and sauerkraut became "freedom slaw" Once again, Pop packed up his family and abalone recipes and moved back to Monterey. (Pat Sands collection.)

Pop initially worked with Gennosuke Kodani and A.M. Allan developing a pre-pounded abalone steak that was sold and shipped to hotels and restaurants all over Northern California. He also developed a method to ship it that kept it fresh for a much longer time. In May 1919, He opened the very first restaurant on the Monterey Wharf. (Pat Sands collection.)

NEAR THE OLD CUSTOM HOUSE   *1919*

THE · CLUB
RESTAURANT

MONTEREY'S SEA FOOD

ABALONE AND **MUSSEL**
SPECIALTIES

''POP'' ERNEST
CHEF

Initially named the Club because it was in the old Monterey Yacht Club, Pop quickly changed the name to Pop Ernest's, where he served abalone steaks, abalone stew, abalone salad, and abalone nectar, which is just the juice that came out of the shell. The local newspaper crowned him the "Abalone King." (Pat Sands collection.)

Pop also had his own abalone dive boat and dive crew. Besides serving his own restaurant, he was brokering abalone all over California. (Pat Sands collection.)

The diver with the camera is Eddie Bushnell, who invented an early underwater camera housing. Bushnell was the diver on Pop's boat as well as a salvage diver and is responsible for laying all the pipes and installing the Monterey sardine hoppers. These hoppers were developed as a floating delivery system for the Monterey sardine canneries. Each hopper was anchored about 500 feet from shore and directly connected to a particular cannery. The boat crews would unload their catch into the hopper, and the fish would be sucked into the cannery at 70 tons an hour. (Bushnell family collection.)

Here, Pop serves his famous abalone stew at his wharf restaurant. He served the stew in the abalone shell, filling up the holes with lead. (Pat Sands collection.)

Because of Pop's recipe, in 1916, the abalone boats brought 600 million tons of red abalone to the Monterey Wharf. By 1920, there were nine Japanese abalone companies operating off the Wharf, and in 1929, the California abalone industry brought in close to $1 million in revenue; 75 percent of that came out of Monterey Bay. (J.B. Phillips Collection, California History Room, Monterey Library.)

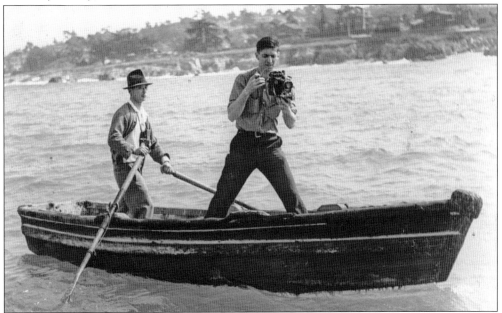

The following photographs were taken in 1938 by two Monterey photographers, Rey Ruppel and Fish and Game biologist J.B. Phillips. Phillips's photographs were taken as a record for Fish and Game. Ruppel, who was a close friend of Monterey abalone diver, Roy Hattori, summited these extraordinary images to *Life* magazine for a possible story. Life liked the idea, especially the photographs, and filed the story away with plans to use them sometime in the near future. On December 7, 1941, Japan attacked Pearl Harbor and the United States entered World War II, so *Life* magazine scraped Rey Ruppel's abalone story. (Photograph by Rey Ruppel, courtesy of the Rey Ruppel Collection, California History Room, Monterey Library.)

Displayed is the typical dive gear used by a Japanese crew. All this gear was manufactured in Japan. The Monterey Japanese divers preferred this Japanese gear over any other gear. Especially the canvas suits. Some divers said they felt like wearing silk. (Photograph by Rey Ruppel, courtesy of the Rey Ruppel Collection, California History Room, Monterey Library.)

Here are the "mother boat" and dive boat. The abalone crews would go out for three days of abalone fishing, sometimes as far as Santa Barbara. These small dive boats were built locally by the Siino Brothers at the Monterey Boat Works. (Rey Ruppel Collection, California History Room, Monterey Library.)

This is then-18-year-old diver Roy Hattori dressed in his wool dive underwear. Hattori was the only Japanese American abalone diver in California at the time. He was born in Monterey in 1920 Nisei, or second generation. All the other divers came from Japan and, for the most part, returned to Japan. (Photograph by Rey Ruppel, courtesy of the Rey Ruppel Collection, California History Room, Monterey Library.)

Roy Hattori learned to dive right after graduating from Monterey High School. His father, Sekisaburo, wanted to get into the abalone business; it was during the Depression, and he thought this would be a good way to make some money, although he had no experience in abalone fishing. He had some friends who were in the abalone business, so he borrowed some equipment and a small boat. (Photograph by Rey Ruppel, courtesy of the Rey Ruppel Collection, California History Room, Monterey Library.)

Sekisaburo took Roy to the middle of the Monterey Harbor, dressed him in the dive gear, and just tossed him overboard. He told him, "You start running down there," and that is how he learned to be an abalone diver. Luckily for Roy, the older divers took him under their wing and showed him what to do. (Photograph by Rey Ruppel, courtesy of the Rey Ruppel Collection, California History Room, Monterey Library.)

Roy Hattori is with his brother James, on the left holding the helmet, and cousin Ishio Enokida, known as "Ish," the boat tender, around 1938. (Photograph by Rey Ruppel, courtesy of the Rey Ruppel Collection, California History Room, Monterey Library.)

Roy Hattori is seen just before his helmet was placed over his head and screwed down to the breastplate. (Rey Ruppel Collection, California History Room, Monterey Library.)

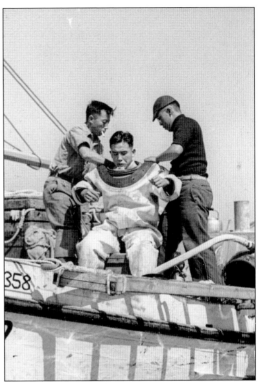

Roy Hattori is on the ladder of the dive boat right before the helmet is attached, getting ready for a fully day of diving abalone. (Rey Ruppel Collection, California History Room, Monterey Library.)

On the right at the stern, or back of the boat, is a Mr. Saki on the sculling oar. The sculling technology came from Japan and was used only by the Japanese. The scull kept the boat in place over the diver without using a motor. The other men on the boat would track the bubbles of the diver. (Photograph by Rey Ruppel, courtesy of the Rey Ruppel Collection, California History Room, Monterey Library.)

Roy Hattori is descending the ladder. The divers usually dove to about 30 feet of water. At that level, they could stay underwater all day without any repercussions; however, some divers would dive as deep as 100 feet. But at that level, there is no light so the diver cannot see anything or stay down there that long. (Photograph by Rey Ruppel, courtesy of the Rey Ruppel Collection, California History Room, Monterey Library.)

The diver would use the ladder when moving to a new diving area. Once the diver is on the ladder, the tender would pull it up so it is level with the boat, and the diver is facing the stern so that when the boat is moving, water will not splash him. (Rey Ruppel Collection, California History Room, Monterey Library.)

Here, Roy Hattori is disappearing into the depths of Monterey Bay. On occasion, Hattori would get the bends, a condition that comes on slowly. He said when that happened, usually at dinner while on the mother boat, the crew would dress him in the gear and put him back in the water on a swing, where he would stay for several hours. Because it was at night, Hattori could not see anything, but he could feel things swimming by and felt like a "big piece of bait." (Rey Ruppel Collection, California History Room, Monterey Library.)

This is a rare photograph of a Monterey abalone boat working near the Point Sur Light station in the Big Sur area, about 30 miles south of Monterey. The diver's hose and bubbles and the man on the scull are visible. This was a favorite spot for the Monterey abalone divers, as they had been diving there since the 1920s. (Rey Ruppel Collection. California History Room, Monterey Library.)

This is a typical day for a Monterey abalone diver: in the water at 9:00 a.m., collect abalone, surface at noon, have lunch, back in the water at 1:00 p.m., collect abalone, and surface at 4:00 p.m. When collected by the diver, the abalone would be put into the abalone basket, a large, knitted bag. In this photograph, the abalone basket is being pulled up by the tender. (Rey Ruppel Collection, California History Room, Monterey Library.)

Diving abalone was a dangerous job. The diver and crew met with all kinds of issues from the bends to bad weather conditions. Roy Hattori was once diving at about 30 feet of water when he got caught in a current that kicked up a rock and cracked the glass on his faceplate. (Rey Ruppel Collection, California History Room, Monterey Library.)

Hattori remembered something an older diver once taught him; he fell flat on his face on the seafloor, reached into his abalone basket, pulled out an abalone, and slid it over his cracked faceplate. The abalone sealed up the crack and stopped the water from coming in. (Rey Ruppel Collection, California History Room, Monterey Library.)

Near the stern of the dive boat is the motor. On top of the housing sits a tea kettle and pair of shoes. Roy Hattori said that he always kept his shoes on the motor housing so that when he came out of the cold water, he could put them on to warm up his feet. And they always had hot water for tea. (Rey Ruppel Collection, California History Room, Monterey Library.)

The abalone season could be a long one, sometimes lasting as much as nine months. Because of Pop Ernest's recipe, by 1920, there were nine Japanese abalone companies operating from the Monterey Wharf and three abalone processing canneries, all Japanese-owned. (Rey Ruppel Collection, California History Room, Monterey Library.)

The boxes on the stern are called "live boxes"; this is technology brought from Japan. These were made locally by the Siino Brothers at the Monterey Boatworks. The boxes are made of redwood, and the abalone would be stacked on top of each other and placed in these boxes. The live boxes were kept in the water for three days, keeping the abalone fresh. (J.B. Phillips Collection, California History Room, Monterey Library.)

After three days of fishing abalone, each boat would come into Monterey with two-hundred dozen large red abalone. They would be unloaded onto the deck of each boat. The boat on the left is waiting to unload at the cannery. (J.B. Phillips Collection, California History Room, Monterey Library.)

The cannery will lower an empty crate and all the abalone is placed into these boxes and pulled directly into the abalone cannery. (J.B. Phillips Collection, California History Room, Monterey Library.)

Almost all the workers in the abalone canneries were Japanese, both men and women. These ladies are separating the abalone by size. (J.B. Phillips Collection, California History Room, Monterey Library.)

These large red abalone are being cut from the shell, the first step in preparation for becoming an abalone steak. (J.B. Phillips Collection, California History Room, Monterey Library.)

Once the abalone is cut from the shell, they are cleaned with fresh water. The man fourth from the left, holding the hose, is diver Roy Hattori. He dove for his family, as they owned their own abalone cannery and, from time to time, worked in a different cannery to make money for fun activities. (J.B. Phillips Collection, California History Room, Monterey Library.)

This woman is trimming the mantle of the abalone and just leaving the foot. The mantle will later be grounded up like hamburger and sold to many local Monterey markets. (J.B. Phillips Collection, California History Room, Monterey Library.)

The abalone foot is then sliced to create the abalone steak. The Hattori abalone cannery had contact with the Pop Ernest restaurant on Monterey Wharf to provide the extra-large steaks. (J.B. Phillips Collection, California History Room, Monterey Library.)

Then on to the pounding tables, a technique invented by Pop Ernest was deployed at his Monterey restaurant in 1908. There was a special way to pound it, so the abalone did not turn into jelly. (J.B. Phillips Collection, California History Room, Monterey Library.)

Seen here is an assembly line of abalone pounders. Men also participated in this operation, and in some cases, they were not all Japanese. Roy Hattori once said that his mother would bring in these big Sicilian guys to "pound the tough steaks." (J.B. Phillips Collection, California History Room, Monterey Library.)

The abalone are being boxed and prepared for shipment to hotels and restaurants all over Northern California. They were shipped on ice by both train and ship. (J.B. Phillips Collection, California History Room, Monterey Library.)

The boxes are ready to be shipped to hotels and restaurants all around Northern California. Abalone had become a very popular menu item, and hotels and restaurants relied on these daily shipments. (Rey Ruppel Collection, California History Room, Monterey Library.)

Pictured is the neon fish sign for the most famous abalone restaurant on the West Coast, Pop Ernest's. (Rey Ruppel Collection, Monterey Library/California Room.)

An abalone steak dinner at Pop's in 1938 was $1.25. That was considered expensive. Some folks would go to Herman's Restaurant, just a few blocks from the wharf, where an abalone steak was just 75¢. (Rey Ruppel Collection, California History Room, Monterey Library.)

A couple is enjoying a special night out at Pop's. In the 1930s, a night out to a restaurant was a very special event, not something you would do every day—or even once a week. An abalone meal then was relatively inexpensive and considered exotic. (Rey Ruppel Collection, California History Room, Monterey Library.)

A large pile of abalone shells is featured. The State of California passed legislation in 1913 restricting the shipment of abalone shells out of the state, so abalone processors on the wharf would just toss the shells into the harbor or truck them out to surrounding towns that were sparsely populated and dump them in the sand dunes. (Rey Ruppel Collection, California History Room, Monterey Library.)

This is an advertisement card for the Salm company. Salm made abalone shell souvenirs starting around the turn of the 20th century that became popular all over the United States. Much of the abalone shell used came from Monterey. (Tim Thomas collection.)

Pictured is a hand-painted leather abalone postcard. At the turn of the 20th century, hand-painted leather postcards were a popular souvenir item. This card would have been made in Monterey. (Inga Waite collection.)

Chinese immigrant abalone fishermen tended to shore-pick abalone or used small boats to navigate between reefs and wash rocks. They would knock the abalone loose from the rocks using poles and wedges and then use a gaff to retrieve them. This brush drawing was created by R.B. Lucas in 1961. (California Department of Fish and Game.)

The process of drying abalone was complex. Once the meat was out of the shell, the meat was cooked, rinsed, and placed in the sun to dry. This specimen is an example of what the finished product looked like. These dried abalone were placed on burlap sacks for transport to the Orient. Following traditional drying methods, this contemporary specimen was produced by abalone processor Scott Westlotorn of Santa Barbara, California. This specimen currently resides in the JCL Heritage Center Museum in Monterey, California. (Steve Rebuck collection.)

At Point Lobos and Cayucos, abalone meat was canned and later shipped to markets. This display is located at the Point Lobos Museum, south of Monterey, California. (Steve Rebuck collection.)

Pictured is the ventral side of a red abalone. *Haliotis rufescens* provided the abalone fishery with the world's largest species and the widest distribution, from Oregon to Baja Mexico. At Morro Bay, for example, landings averaged two million pounds annually from 1916 until the early 1960s—a very sustainable fishery. This specimen was taken by George Koremetis of Morro Bay, California, on April 1, 1956. (Glen Bickford collection.)

Two

ABALONE SPECIES

This specimen of red abalone, *Haliotis rufescens*, shows a "dietary tag," commonly known as candy stripes. In some areas, abalone would consume a variety of seaweeds or kelps. These algae could be blue, green, white, brown, or red. The animal would lay down a layer of new shell growth with a corresponding color. (Steve Rebuck collection.)

This fossilized abalone, *Haliotis lomaensis*, from Point Loma, California, is 12.8 mm long, 9.0 mm wide, and 3.0 mm high. (California Academy of Sciences, California Department of Fish and Game.)

This specimen of *Haliotis wallallensis* (common name "flat abalone") in sandstone is found at Cayucos, California. (Steve Rebuck collection.)

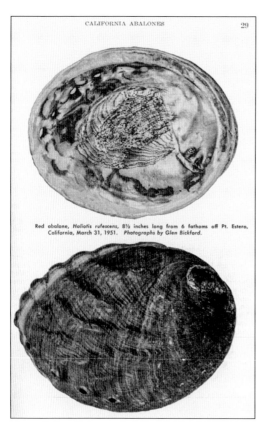

Red abalone, *Haliotis rufescens*, 8½ inches long from 6 fathoms off Pt. Estero, California, March 31, 1951. *Photographs by Glen Bickford.*

Red abalone, *Haliotis rufescens*, Swainson, 1822, are the world's largest of 140 different species. The largest documented individual specimen is 12.25 inches in diameter. Holes average two to four. Distribution of this species is from Sunset Bay, Oregon, to Turtle Bay, Baja California, Mexico. Red abalone are also common on the northern and southern Channel Island offshore Southern California. Habitat is rocky nearshore, high tide where they are most plentiful between 20 to 50 feet sea water. The highest quantities were found from Cape San Martin to Morro Bay. (California Department of Fish and Game.)

Pink abalone, *Haliotis corrugata*, 6⅝ inches long from 10 fathoms off La Jolla, California, February 26, 1952. *Photographs by Glen Bickford.*

Pink abalone, *Haliotis corrugata*, Gray, 1828. After red abalone, pinks were the most harvested. Pink abalone have thick, circular, high-arched shells measuring up to 10 inches. Holes range from two to seven. Distribution is between Point Conception, Santa Barbara County, California, to Turtle Bay, Baja California, Mexico. On the Channel Islands, they are most common to San Clemente and Santa Barbara Islands, primarily in 20 to 80 feet sea water, in exposed coastline with active surf. (California Department of Fish and Game.)

Green abalone, *Haliotis fulgens*, Phillipi, 1845, have multicolor, green interior shells, brick red on the exterior and can measure up to 10 inches with five to seven holes. Distribution is Point Conception, Santa Barbara County, California, to Magdalena Bay, Baja California, Mexico. Habitat is rocky nearshore low tide to 25 feet sea water, but they may be found as deep as 50 feet sea water. Most common in 10 to 20 feet sea water. (California Department of Fish and Game.)

Green abalone, *Haliotis fulgens*, 7 inches long from 1 fathom off Long Point, Santa Catalina Island, February 22, 1952. *Photographs by Glen Bickford.*

Black abalone, *Haliotis cracherodii*. Top: 3½ inches long from intertidal zone, Catalina Harbor, Santa Catalina Island, California. Bottom: 3⅝ inches long from intertidal zone, Catalina Harbor, Santa Catalina Island, California. *Photographs by Glen Bickford.*

Black abalone, *Haliotis cracherodii*, Leach, 1817, have smooth shells, generally black in color, but may have bands of blue or red. Holes number from five to nine and they may reach slightly more than eight inches in length. Distribution is from Coos Bay, Oregon, to Cape San Lucas, Baja California, Mexico. Habitat is from the high tide mark to 20 feet sea water. Black abalone are often found in large quantities with individuals stacked on top of one another. Subspecies are common. Black abalone were listed as an endangered species on January 14, 2009. (California Department of Fish and Game.)

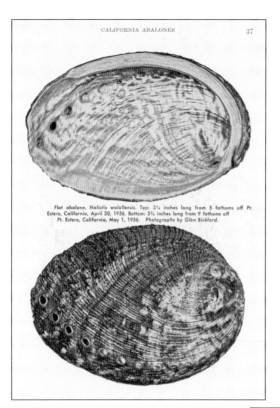

Flat abalone, *Haliotis walallensis*. Top: 3¼ inches long from 5 fathoms off Pt. Estero, California, April 30, 1956. Bottom: 3½ inches long from 9 fathoms off Pt. Estero, California, May 1, 1956. *Photographs by Glen Bickford.*

Flat abalone, *Haliotis wallallensis*, Stearns, 1899. Shells are oval, long, narrow and flat with four to eight holes. Length is three to five inches. Distribution is from British Columbia, Canada, to La Jolla, California. Although rare south of Carmel, California, they are somewhat common in San Luis Obispo County, California. Flat abalone habitat is from subtidal to 70 feet sea water. These abalone sometimes congregate with other species. (California Department of Fish and Game.)

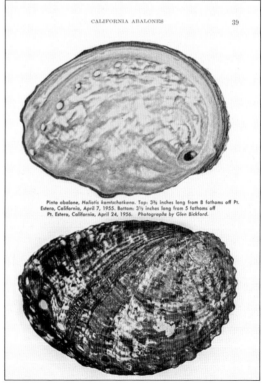

Pinto abalone, *Haliotis kamtschatkana*. Top: 3¼ inches long from 8 fathoms off Pt. Estero, California, April 7, 1955. Bottom: 3½ inches long from 5 fathoms off Pt. Estero, California, April 24, 1956. *Photographs by Glen Bickford.*

Pinto abalone, *Haliotis kamtschatkana*, Jonas, 1845, have long and narrow shells, four to six inches, with three to six holes. Distribution is from Sitka, Alaska, to Point Conception, Santa Barbara County, California. A subspecies is known in Japan. Some scientists see threaded abalone, *H. assimilis*, as a subspecies of *H. kamtschatkana*. Habitat in Alaska is shallow and deeper southward. Pinto abalone are common in San Luis Obispo County from 35 to 50 feet sea water. (California Department of Fish and Game.)

White abalone, *Haliotis sorenseni*, Bartsch 1940, have relatively thin, light, oval, and highly arched shells, with three to five "fluted" holes, with size up to 10 inches. Their distribution is south of Point Conception, Santa Barbara County, California, to San Diego, California, and the southern Channel Islands, with reports of Turtle Island, Baja California, Mexico. White abalone habitat extends from 15 feet sea water to 150 feet sea water, with the greatest concentrations at 80 to 100 feet sea water. White abalone were listed as an endangered species in May 2001. (California Department of Fish and Game.)

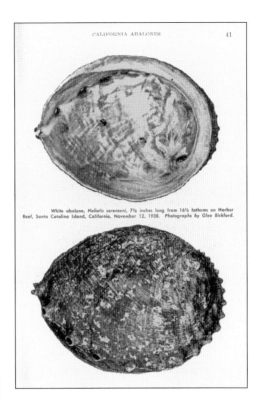

White abalone, *Haliotis sorenseni*, 7½ inches long from 16½ fathoms on Harbor Reef, Santa Catalina Island, California, November 12, 1958. *Photographs by Glen Bickford.*

Threaded abalone, *Haliotis assimilis*, 5 inches long from 12 fathoms off Pt. Loma, California, June 1955. *Photographs by Glen Bickford.*

Threaded abalone, *Haliotis assimilis*, Dall, 1878, have relatively thin, oval shells. Some, approximately five percent, have striking multicolor bands of blue, green, white, orange, and red known as "banded assimilis." Threaded abalone grow to four to six inches with four to six holes. Distribution is from Point Conception, Santa Barbara County, California, to Turtle Bay, Baja California, Mexico. Large populations once occurred near Point Estero, San Luis Obispo County, California. Habitat is from 10 feet sea water to over 120 feet sea water with greatest numbers from 70 feet sea water to 100 feet sea water. (California Department of Fish and Game.)

This is the dorsal side of a red abalone, *Haliotis rufescens*. At various times, abalone shells have been more valuable than the meat. A variety of items from jewelry to buttons were manufactured from abalone shells. The abalone shell has three layers. Designers of modern military combat armor and helmets have copied the structure of abalone shells to make personal protective equipment more effective. (Glen Bickford collection.)

Abalone in the wild tend to congregate into dense populations, which enhances their ability to successfully spawn and reproduce. (Jeffery Baldwin collection.)

Mortality in the wild is an important observation. It is a way to gauge the overall health of a population. These specimens were collected by Glen Bickford during Keith Cox surveys from White Point, near La Jolla, the site of Montrose Chemical DDT waste disposal. (Glen Bickford collection.)

Three

ABALONE RESEARCH

Field research conducted by the California Department of Fish and Game began at the turn of the 20th century. Here, biologist Keith Cox (left) is being tended by Glen Bickford (right). The last step before submerging is to mount the helmet on the breastplate and lock it down. (Glen Bickford collection.)

Biologist Keith Cox is on the ladder preparing to dive. The marine environment can be a hostile place to work. Basically, one enters the food chain. These men had to prepare as underwater "gladiators" to survive their day at the office. (Glen Bickford collection.)

Another important component of successful diving is a competent boat operator. In this case, William "Pinky" Thomas was the man. (Glen Bickford collection.)

Heavy-gear diver Keith Cox examines abalone on top of a rock in the wild. When abalone sense disturbance, they suck down on the rock with their powerful foot. This image was captured in Avalon, Santa Catalina Island, on September 28, 1957. (Glen Bickford collection.)

Not only did the Cox research team use heavy diving gear, but they also experimented with early SCUBA gear. The diver is identified as "Aqua Lung (Pete)." (Glen Bickford collection.)

The Cox research team would use one to six divers to accomplish their tasks. (Glen Bickford collection.)

SCUBA (Self Contained Underwater Breathing Apparatus) was a new technology in the 1950s. Keith Cox was an early user of SCUBA in his abalone research. Here, two divers conduct underwater research on a naturally occurring reef. (Glen Bickford collection.)

Onboard, the research people would measure, weigh, sex, and tag their specimens. Some tagged abalone that would later be recovered. The attached data would identify any growth of the animal. (Glen Bickford collection.)

Research was also international. Here, Japanese minister of fisheries Takashi Ono and Keith Cox discuss abalone resources at Fort Bragg, California, in 1954. (Glen Bickford collection.)

Not all research was conducted underwater, Here, biologist Keith Cox examines and measures an abalone near was rock on the beach. The team was tagging red abalone on the beach at Olsen's Ranch, near Gualala, on June 3, 1954. (Glen Bickford collection.)

The Keith Cox research team surveys inshore rocks during studies in the late 1950s. They are seen tagging red abalone on the beach at Olsen's Ranch, near Gualala on June 3, 1954. (Glen Bickford collection.)

California Department of Fish and Game used a variety of different sized boat in their marine research. Here are four vessels of various sizes from near 200 feet to 32 feet in size. This vessel strategy offered researchers different options for moving equipment and personnel to various inshore/offshore sites. (Glen Bickford collection.)

From field research, state, academic, and civilian biologists found ways to spawn and settle abalone in raceways. Some of these juveniles were released back into the wild or grown out to a harvestable size as a commercial food source. (Jeffery Baldwin collection.)

Another form of abalone aquaculture at the Abalone Farm, Cayucos, California, founded in 1969, uses a laboratory, raceways, and tubes to grow its abalone. Commercial divers would purchase seed abalone for "outplanting." (Steve Rebuck collection.)

In the 1970s, the California Department of Fish and Game experimented with the outplanting of abalone. Here, CDFG biologist Richard Burge prepares for a dive during the planting of up to 40,000 juvenile abalone at San Miguel Island, Santa Barbara County, California. (Richard Burge collection.)

A decade later, in the mid-1980s, the commercial abalone diver members of the California Abalone Association also began outplanting juvenile abalone. Here, Laddie Handelman prepares to dive and release juveniles at San Miguel Island, Santa Barbara County, California. (Bob Evans Designs.)

Four

DIVING THE SOUTH-CENTRAL COAST

In 1928, the Pierce Brothers acquired a diving dress, helmet, and air pump and began fishing abalone. In this photograph, diver Bill Pierce is "dressed in" and preparing to walk into the surf, over rocks, wearing approximately 150 pounds of equipment, and return with 70–100 pounds of abalone. Another brother operates a hand-powered air pump. It was reported that the next season, the Pierce Brothers had a boat. (Pierce family collection.)

Diver William Pierce remeasures his abalone while resting on the deck. Size limits were strictly enforced so it was common practice to remeasure on deck any questionable abalone. Double-checking was very important. Game wardens often check abalone for legal size, on deck, or when delivered to port. (Glen Bickford collection.)

A. Paladini Company of San Francisco was a fish processing and distribution center. The Pierce Brothers operated their abalone processing business out of the Paladini Building on Monterey St., Morro Bay. (Glen Bickford collection.)

An obviously exhausted Glen Bickford is dressed in his dive suit onboard his boat in about 1940. (Glen Bickford collection.)

Seen here are Al and Norma Hanson, with Al dressed in. The Hansons began their abalone diving and processing careers at Cambria, California, in 1945. (Glen Bickford collection.)

Commercial diver Laddie Handelman is on the ladder preparing for a dive, with tender Bill Pouch assisting. (Barney Clancy collection.)

Laddie Handelman is preparing to dive, now wearing his helmet. Note how his dive suit (dress) is "ballooned" up, filled with air. Once a diver is in the water, he uses an exhaust valve inside the helmet to release excess air by leaning his head against the valve. To ascend, the diver once again allows the suit to inflate with air, and he will rise to the surface. (Barney Clancy collection.)

When a diver returns to port, he first ties up his boat at his processor's dock. The abalone are then placed in boxes or totes and hoisted into the processing shop. This is the F/V *Katherine K.*, owned by George "the Greek" Kouremetis at Brebes Oceanhouse, Morro Bay, California, around 1960. (Glen Bickford collection.)

The abalone were unloaded from the boxes and placed on tables. Next steps included shucking the abalone from their shells, washing them, and preparing them for trimming and slicing into steaks. Each abalone weighs between 3.5 and 5 pounds. (Glen Bickford collection.)

Next, the meat was "punched out" of the shells. The abalone meat is attached inside the shell. The meat yield was approximately 30 percent of the abalone's total weight. A small bar resembling a chisel was used in this process to dislodge the meat from the shell. (Glen Bickford collection.)

The abalone were next placed in cement mixes for a bath to remove any sand or other debris and then moved to a settling table. The abalone would stay on this table overnight, allowing them time to relax their muscle tissue. (Glen Bickford collection.)

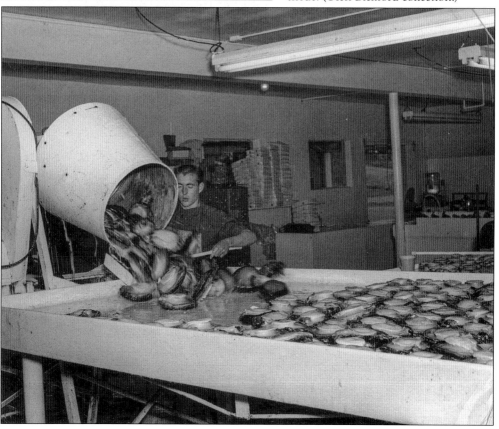

Settling overnight causes the abalone meat to relax. Abalone meat is solid muscle. Settling helped soften the flesh so it could more easily be trimmed and sliced into steaks. (Glen Bickford collection.)

The mantle of the abalone the dark black band of meat around the foot is trimmed away with sharp knives. The abalone market preferred the bright white meat. Some abalone meat could be tan and was labeled as "golden" for marketing purposes. (Glen Bickford collection.)

Up-trimming removes hard pieces of the abalone foot. Old clawfoot bathtubs were used to further wash the abalone in preparation for slicing into steaks. (Glen Bickford collection.)

The abalone meat is being sliced into steaks. This technique revolutionized the marketing of abalone into the restaurant staple it became. This process help make the steak easier to handle and package into a marketable product. (Glen Bickford collection.)

The final step in processing abalone was to pound the steaks with heavy wooden mallets. The intent is to further "shock" the tissue into relaxing, making it more tender. (Glen Bickford collection.)

The processed abalone steaks are next placed into five-pound waxed cardboard boxes. These boxes were the invention of Frank Brebes of Morro Bay. Prior to this, abalone were shipped in wooden boxes, which were very messy. (Glen Bickford collection.)

Pictured are a few examples of colorful and personalized waxed cardboard boxes. These boxes were widely used, relatively durable, and have now become collectors items themselves. (Steve Rebuck collection.)

Loading their pickup, another family from the Azores was the Sylvester family. These men worked out of Port San Luis, San Luis Obispo County, around the 1950s. (Colleen Gnos collection.)

The Sylvester family continued to dive for abalone and fish for salmon while also founding Sylvester Tug Service, where they serviced oil tankers at Port San Luis, Morro Bay, and Cayucos. (Colleen Gnos collection.)

Ocean View Cafe
AVILA, CALIFORNIA

a-la-Carte

Fried Filet of Sole	1.25
Fried Shrimps	1.50
Fried Halibut	1.25
Fried Ling Cod	1.40
Abalone Steak	1.50

POTATOES, SALAD, BREAD & BUTTER SERVED WITH ABOVE ORDERS

Chicken Fried Steak	1.25
Baby Beef Liver, with onions	1.25
2 Fried Pork Chops	1.25
Lamb Chops	1.25
Hamburger Steak	1.00
Ham Steak	1.25
Tenderloin Steak	2.25
Baked Sugar Cured Ham	1.50
Fried Chicken	1.75
Shrimp Cocktail	.50
CHILI & BEANS	.50
CLAM CHOWDER	.50

This menu from the 1950s for Ocean View Café in Avila Beach, California, demonstrates the relative commonality of abalone at somewhat reasonable prices. At this time, commercial divers were paid approximately 50¢ each for an eight-inch diameter red abalone. (Steve Rebuck collection.)

Earnest "Skinner" Pierce was one of the top divers at Morro Bay in the 1950s. He became a Caterpillar tractor operator (Cat-Skinner), thus his nickname. He died in a Big Sur, Highway 1, landslide in 1983. His body has never been recovered. (Glen Bickford collection.)

Beginning with the Japanese immigrant abalone fishermen, heavy diving gear was introduced in about 1860. These divers spent many hours per day underwater selecting their catch and sending it to the surface. Although cumbersome, this gear was warm and dry. Under the canvas dive dress, the diver typically wore wool clothing and could layer up with sweaters, The suit with helmet and weights weighed approximately 150 pounds. (Glen Bickford collection.)

Heavy-gear diving equipment took considerable strength and fortitude to operate and negotiate. Al Hanson and Dr. John Craig are pictured in Avalon, Santa Catalina Island, in 1958. Dr. Craig had a 1950s TV show, *Danger is My Business.* (Glen Bickford collection.)

Al Hanson and Dr. John Craig are filming *Danger is My Business.* Hanson's episode demonstrated one cutting themselves out of a flooded dive dress. He said later that it was "the stupidest thing I ever did." (Glen Bickford collection.)

Delmar "Foozie" Riviea of Morro Bay, California, is dressed in and "riding the ladder." (Glen Bickford collection.)

Foozie Reviea is being tended to and dressed. This would be a typical lunchtime view. The diver is Delmar Reviea, the line tender is Doug Reviea, and the boat skinner is Buddy Reviea. (Glen Bickford collection.)

Line tender Doug Reviea is pulling up the "Barney bag" full of abalone from brother and diver Delmar Reviea above Pt Estero. (Glen Bickford collection.)

Delmar Reviea is on the ladder preparing to exit the water. Abalone diving was hard work. Not only was the gear heavy and cumbersome, but also the water ranged from the high 40 degrees to mid-50 degrees. Wool clothing under the "dive dress" kept divers warm even when wet. A walking diver might cover more than a mile underwater during a day's work. (Glen Bickford collection.)

Delmar Reviea is abalone diving above Point Estero (near Cayucos, northern San Luis Obispo County, California), exiting the water with assistance from brother and line tender, Doug Reviea. (Glen Bickford collection.)

Five

DIVE EQUIPMENT AND TOOLS

This is a nice example of a commercial abalone pry bar. Automotive leaf spring was the chosen material for this tool. It also has a caliper attached as required by law for measuring one's abalone catch. This bar was owned by commercial abalone diver George "the Greek" Koremetis of Morro Bay. (Courtesy Tam Munro, Steve Rebuck collection.)

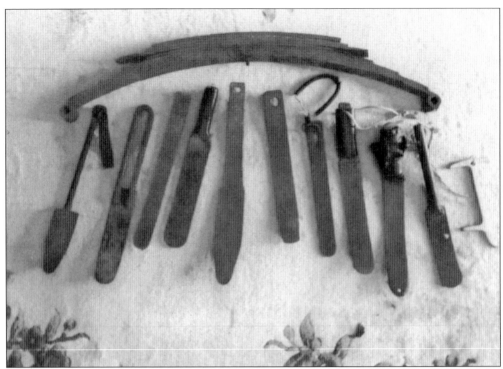

Pictured is a collection of leaf spring abalone pry bars. Note the Model T leaf spring component, the base material used for these bars, in the background. (Steve Rebuck collection.)

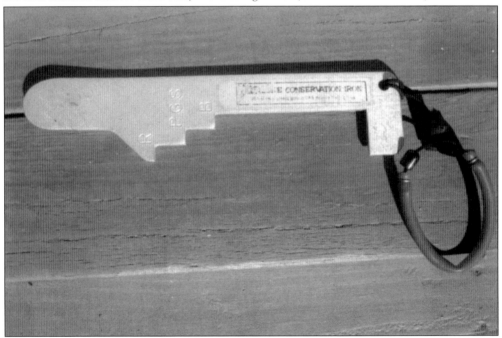

Commercial members of the California Abalone Association invented this "conservation bar" similar to a commercial bar to help reduced "bar cuts." Abalone are hemophiliacs and will die if cut. (Photograph by Steve Rebuck.)

In this 1966 image, diver Bob McMillen is wearing an early wet suit, mask, fins, and an air system that became known as "Hookah." State regulations require that a diver remain attached to his boat. This was accomplished through the diver's air hose, which varied in length from 200 feet to several hundred feet. (Bob McMillen collection.)

Back on deck, Bob McMillen shows off some of the larger red abalone specimens he had collected from his "secret spot" at Santa Rosa Island. 125 dozen red abalone. McMillen used this gear for an estimated 40,000 hours or 4.5 years underwater. (Bob McMillen collection.)

This new technology was picked up by commercial and recreational abalone divers for the next 60-plus years. In this 1985 photograph, commercial diver Mike Radon sits on his boat's gunnel wearing a custom-made wet suit and "jet fins." (Steve Rebuck collection.)

Commercial abalone diver, Mike Radon remeasures his catch before "putting them to bed" in the live well on his boat F/V *Allyson Way* in 1985. (F/V signifies "Fishing Vessel.") (Steve Rebuck collection.)

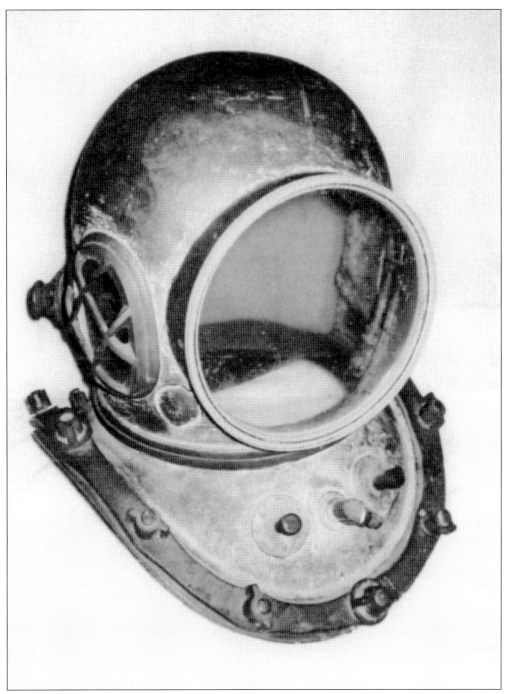

Japanese (Yokohama Diving Apparatus, Ltd.) commercial diving helmets were first used to dive abalone in California in about 1896. This example belonged to Morro Bay commercial abalone diver Ed Pierce. It was modified as many were with a larger viewing port (light). These helmets were most preferred due to their relatively lighter weight. In addition, the helmet's breastplate was somewhat wider, providing additional comfort as a diver would lean forward while searching for and picking abalone. (Steve Rebuck collection.)

This Japanese Nippon dive helmet also has a modified light (viewport) in the front for better vision. This example belonged to commercial abalone diver Frank Brebes of Morro Bay. While Japanese helmets were favored due to their light weight, Greek sponge helmets were also used. (Steve Rebuck collection.)

Six

ABALONE DIVE BOATS

This abalone dive boat was identified by the photographer as "a typical abalone boat of the 1930s." (Glen Bickford collection.)

A diver and crew are aboard F/V *28X288*, Glen Bickford's personal boat before he sold it to the Department of Fish and Game in 1948. (Glen Bickford collection.)

This is a view of the starboard (right) side of the F/V *28X288*. The A-11 number is one sequentially given by the California Department of Fish and Game for all commercial abalone dive boats. A small "house" (living quarters for overnight trips) has been added. (Glen Bickford collection.)

Another commercial abalone dive boat, A-24 is featured with a ladder attached to the vessel. These ladders identified the vessel as a "heavy gear dive boat." (Glen Bickford collection.)

This example of an abalone dive boat, A-39 is more of the traditional style of an American commercial fishing boat. Following World War II, many other types of boats were used in the abalone fishery. (Glen Bickford collection.)

1940

OB GLASS LINE TENDER, LANKY TIPTON DIVER, WIMPY PIERCE OPERATO

This Japanese Siino boat was owned by the Pierce Brothers, pictured with diver Lanky Tipton in 1940. (Pierce family collection.)

Al and Norma Hanson are aboard their boat F/V *Geanie* around 1946, Santa Catalina Island, California. The Hansons acquired this boat at Cambria in 1945 and then moved to Santa Catalina Island. (Glen Bickford collection.)

Seen here is the F/V *Northwind*, at Avalon, Santa Catalina Island, in 1947. It is an example of a World War II Higgins LCVP (Landing Craft Vehicle Personnel) fabricated for commercial fishing by George Eldon Rebuck. What appear to be white flags are actually baby diapers. (Steve Rebuck collection.)

F/V *Laura Bell* is seen in San Diego in 1951. This boat too was a modified Higgins LCVP. Fabrication by George Eldon Rebuck. The *Northwind* and *Laura Bell* were both purchased from war surplus. (Steve Rebuck collection.)

Another Higgins landing craft, this one a Eureka boat, the F/V *Spoonbill* owned by Bob and Ted Benton of Santa Barbara. F/V *Spoonbill* was also the name for this model of a 36-foot Higgins boat. (Bob and Ted Benton collection.)

This example of a Higgins Eureka was the F/V *Andelea*. Onboard are, from left to right, "Big John" Pierce, Laddie Handelman, and Bill Bossert in about 1960. This boat was painted in the traditional Black Fleet colors: black with red trim. (Barney Clancy collection.)

This Higgins Eureka was F/V *Genes Folly*, which fished the Morro Bay areas north in the late 1950s and early 1960s with diver Bob Colomy. (Earnie Porter collection.)

Black Fleet owner Barney Clancy typically had a fleet of five boats. This one, F/V *Cathie*, was Laddie Handelman's boat in the late 1950s and early 1960s. This boat fished abalone in the Morro Bay area. Handelman, originally from New York City, came to California at age 17 to fish abalone with his uncle Jimmy Perog. (Barney Clancy collection.)

F/V *Nina* was another Barney Clancy Black Fleet boat, the smallest of his fleet. Clancy worked this boat from San Diego to southern Monterey County. Clancy had a quota of 200 dozen abalone per week per boat, so rich was the abalone resource at this time. (Barney Clancy collection.)

This is a view if the bow of the F/V *Cathie* while the "tender" is preparing the abalone diver equipment. This function is called "dressing-in." Removing one's dive gear is called "dressing-out." The boat operator keeps the boat steady during this process. (Barney Clancy collection.)

The dive tender assists his diver on the ladder on the Black Fleet F/V *Lorraine W.* The diver would sometime "ride-the-ladder" while the boat operator moved to another location. This could be dangerous and required extreme care to prevent injuring the diver. (Barney Clancy collection.)

The Black Fleet, owned by processor Barney Clancy, is shown tied up at Morro Bay in about 1955. This collection, generally sport boats modified for commercial diving, ventured north from Wilmington, California. Clancy had worked the area in 1946 after working at the Hayward, California, shipyards building Liberty ships for the war effort. Clancy bought paint from war surplus stores and painted his fleet black with red trim. (Barney Clancy collection.)

Abalone diver Ernest Porter of Morro Bay and boat operator and business partner Dean Tyler owned and operated this smaller commercial abalone boat, F/V *Cindy*, in the early 1960s–1970s. (Ernie Porter collection.)

Commercial diver Earnie Porter's F/V *Easy* was a homemade boat built in that transition period between the larger three-man crew boats and the shift in the 1960s to two-man crews. (Richard Burge collection.)

In the early 1960s, commercial abalone diver and boat designer/builder, Ron Radon began building a new style of commercial abalone dive boar, the Radoncraft. These boats featured a new invention: a rear engine and stern-drive transmission. These boats were lighter and faster, using V-8 gasoline engines. (Don Radon, D.R. Radon Boatbuilding.)

Small and compact, these Radon boats revolutionized abalone diving especially when the commercial abalone fishery shifted to the Northern Channel Islands in the 1970s and 1980s. Cuddy cabins and stand-up controls made rough water easier to navigate. (Photograph by Steve Rebuck.)

Another example of the Radon boat is this one with the forward cuddy cabin and stand-up controls. For transiting the Santa Barbara Channel, which could be rough, standing up while driving the boat was far more comfortable. (Steve Rebuck collection.)

At Dutch Harbor, San Nicolas Island (SNI), seven commercial abalone boats are side-tied and ready to go to work on July 31, 1984. The boats are the *Sonrisa*, *Santa Rosa*, *Aint Right*, *Malaea*, *Orta Vez*, *Rancho Delux*, and *R. Jean*. The divers and crew were made up of Mark Becker, Kenny Schmidt, John Becker, Mark Connelly, Norm Graziano, Bobby McKinley, Dino Cripps, John Colgate, Norm Couture, Chris Hawkins, Curt Petterson, Jim Marshall, Dave Rauch, Thierry Brown, Doug Grover, Tom Hallahan, and Bob Askew. At this time, approximately 41 percent of all commercial abalone landings were originating from SNI. In 1987, the US Fish and Wildlife Service began an experimental translocation of sea otters to SNI. Within three years (1990), commercial red abalone landings from SMI declined to three percent. (Photograph by George Tomlinson.)

In Northern California, north of San Francisco, SCUBA and Hookah are prohibited. Only "freediving" (holding one breath) is allowed. South of San Francisco, surface supplied air: heavy gear, hookah, and/or SCUBA is allowed. (Photograph by Ken Bailey, Seadreams Productions.)

A recreational diver using a snorkel has found a few abalone and approaches with a picking bar and flashlight. (Photograph by Ken Bailey, Seadreams Productions.)

A recreational diver has selected an abalone and is using a caliper to measure it before harvesting, as mandated by State of California law. (Photograph by Ken Bailey, Seadreams Productions.)

This is another image of a recreational diver searching for abalone with a flashlight and utilizing a caliper to measure his findings. (Photograph by Ken Bailey, Seadreams Productions.)

Recreational diver Matt Lum of Santa Barbara stands with the reward: a red abalone nearly 11 inches in diameter. An abalone of this size may have five or six pounds of recoverable meat. (Matt Lum collection.)

Seven

TECHNOLOGY INFLUENCED BY ABALONE DIVERS

After his abalone diving career, commercial diver Laddies Handelman was involved in the development of mixed gas diving. This technology allows divers to breathe a mixture of gasses where nitrogen is removed and replaced with helium. In this photograph, Handelman is entering a diving chamber where his body is pressured to his last diving depth, then slowly depressurized back to surface pressure. A diver is limited to a three week-cycle of diving, pressurization, and ultimate decompression. Dives of this manner today are to depths over 100 feet sea water. (Lad Handelman collection.)

The Kirby-Morgan Corporation was founded by two former commercial abalone divers, Robert Kirby and Bev Morgan, and currently commands 75 percent of the worldwide market on dive helmet production. They are located in Santa Maria, California. (Robert Kirby collection.)

The Kirby-Morgan Corporation also built state-of-the-art air system regulators. Pictured is the Kirby-Morgan SuperFlow 350. (Kirby-Morgan Corporation.)

Another helmet designer and former commercial abalone diver is Robert Ratcliffe of Santa Barbara, California. Ratcliffe designed the Rat Hat in the 1960s. He was also a co-founder of Oceaneering International, Inc. NASA and Oceaneering Space Solutions are now developing a space helmet for the US trip to Mars. (Robert Ratcliffe collection.)

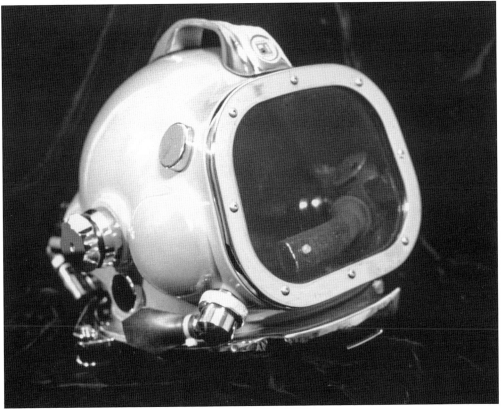

Featured is a Rat Hat diver. Hookah dive equipment was developed by commercial abalone divers from around 1960 forward. The Rat Hat used today with commercial dive gear demonstrates the evolution of equipment. (Robert Ratcliffe collection.)

The Newtsuit was designed by Phil Nuytten of Nuytco Research in British Columbia. This suit can be purchased by a civilian, mounted on an A-frame, and a diver can descend in 1,000 feet sea water. (Courtesy Phil Nuytten, Nuytco Research LTD.)

BIBLIOGRAPHY

Bonnot, Paul. *The Abalones of California*. California Department of Fish and Game, 1948.

Cox, Keith W. *California Abalones, Family Haliotidae*. California Department of Fish and Game, 1962.

Croker, R.S. *Abalones*. California Department of Fish and Game, 1931.

Edwards, Charles Lincoln. *The Abalone Industry of California*. California Department of Fish and Game, 1913.

Fanshawe, Samantha, G.R. VanBlaricom, A.A. Shelly. *Restoring Top Carnivores as Detriments to the Performance of Marine Protected Areas Intended for Fishery Stability: A Case Study with Red Abalones and Sea Otters*. Conservation Biology, 2003.

Geiger, Daniel L., Buzz Owen,.*Abalone-Worldwide Haliotidae*. Conch Books, 2012.

Hanson, Alfred, N.J. Hanson. *More Than Nine Lives: An Autobiography of a Life Well Lived*. Footprint, 2003.

Kirby, Robert. *Hard Hat Divers Wear Dresses*. Olive Press, 2002.

Lundy, A.L. "Scrap," *The California Abalone Industry: A Pictorial History*. Best Publishing Company, 1996.

Lydon, Sandy. *Chinese Gold: The Chinese in the Monterey Bay Region*. Capitola Book Company, 2008. Monterey Maritime Museum. *Gennosuke Kodoni and the Abalone Fishermen from Chiba, Japan Who Introduced Diving Methods into California*. J.B. Phillips Historical Fisheries Report, 2007.

Phillips, J.B. *Abalone*. California Department of Fish and Game, 1937.

Thomas, Tim. *The Abalone King of Monterey*. The History Press, 2014.

Wild, Paul W., J.A. Ames. *A Report on the Sea Otter*, Enhydra lutris l. *in California*. California Department of Fish and Game, 1974.

Yamada, David Takao. *The Japanese of the Monterey Peninsula: Their History and Legacy 1895–1995*. Monterey County Japanese American Citizens League, 1995.

DISCOVER THOUSANDS OF LOCAL HISTORY BOOKS
FEATURING MILLIONS OF VINTAGE IMAGES

Arcadia Publishing, the leading local history publisher in the United States, is committed to making history accessible and meaningful through publishing books that celebrate and preserve the heritage of America's people and places.

Find more books like this at
www.arcadiapublishing.com

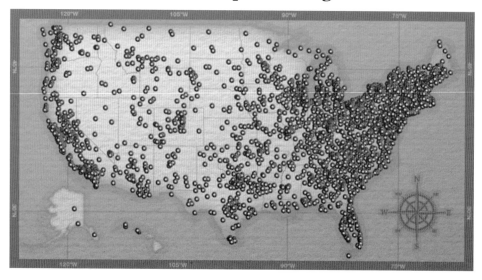

Search for your hometown history, your old stomping grounds, and even your favorite sports team.

Consistent with our mission to preserve history on a local level, this book was printed in South Carolina on American-made paper and manufactured entirely in the United States. Products carrying the accredited Forest Stewardship Council (FSC) label are printed on 100 percent FSC-certified paper.

MADE IN THE USA